21st
Century
Skills Library

COOL SCIENCE CAREERS

BIOENGINEER

SUSAN H. GRAY

Published in the United States of America by Cherry Lake Publishing, Ann Arbor, Michigan www.cherrylakepublishing.com

Content Advisers
University of Illinois
- Rashid Bashir, PhD, Director, Micro and Nanotechnology Laboratory, and Professor of Electrical and Computer Engineering, and Bioengineering
- Irfan S. Ahmad, PhD, Associate Director, Center for Nanoscale Science and Technology, and Research Faculty, Agricultural and Biological Engineering
- Jimmy Hsia, PhD, Professor of Mechanical Science and Engineering, and Director for Education and Outreach, Center on Emergent Behaviors of Integrated Cellular Systems

Massachusetts Institute of Technology
Roger Kamm, PhD, Director, NSF Science and Technology Center on Emergent Behaviors of Integrated Cellular Systems, and Professor of Mechanical Engineering, and Bioengineering

Georgia Institute of Technology
Robert Nerem, PhD, Professor of Biomedical Engineering

Photo Credits
Cover and pages 1 and 20, courtesy of Department of Bioengineering, University of Illinois; page 4, ©iStockphoto.com/Rolphus; pages 6, 8, courtesy of Brian Cunningham research group at Micro and Nanotechnology Laboratory, University of Illinois; page 10 and 27, courtesy of Roger Kamm research group, Department of Biological Engineering, Massachusetts Institute of Technology; page 12, courtesy of Rashid Bashir research group at Micro and Nanotechnology Lab., University of Illinois; pages 13 and 15, courtesy of InvoTek, Inc. of Alma, Arkansas; pages 16, 19, and 28 courtesy of Micro and Nanotechnology Laboratory, University of Illinois; page 21, ©michaeljung/Shutterstock, Inc.; page 23, courtesy of Bionanotechology Laboratory/Micro and Nanotechnology Laboratory, University of Illinois; page 24, courtesy of Georgia Institute of Technology.

Program Sponsors
- NSF-funded Science and Technology Center on Emergent Behaviors of Integrated Cellular Systems (STC-EBICS)
- NSF-funded Integrative Graduate Education and Research Traineeship on Cellular and Molecular Mechanics and BioNanotechnology (IGERT-CMMB)
- NCI-funded Midwest Cancer Nanotechnology Training Center (M-CNTC)
- University of Illinois Center for Nanoscale Science and Technology (CNST) collaboratory

Library of Congress Cataloging-in-Publication Data
Gray, Susan H.
  Bioengineer/By Susan H. Gray.
    p. cm.—(Cool science careers)
  Includes bibliographical references and index.
  ISBN-13: 978-1-61080-035-8 (lib. bdg.)
  ISBN-10: 1-61080-035-4 (lib. bdg.)
  1. Bioengineering—Vocational guidance—Juvenile literature. I. Title.
  TA164.G73 2011
  610.28—dc22   2010039483

Cherry Lake Publishing would like to acknowledge the work of The Partnership for 21st Century Skills. Please visit *www.21stcenturyskills.org* for more information.

Printed in the United States of America at Corporate Graphics Inc.
January 2011
CLSP08

TABLE OF CONTENTS

CHAPTER ONE
BIOLOGY PLUS ENGINEERING

Do you know anyone who uses a hearing aid? Does someone in your class wear contact lenses? Do you have

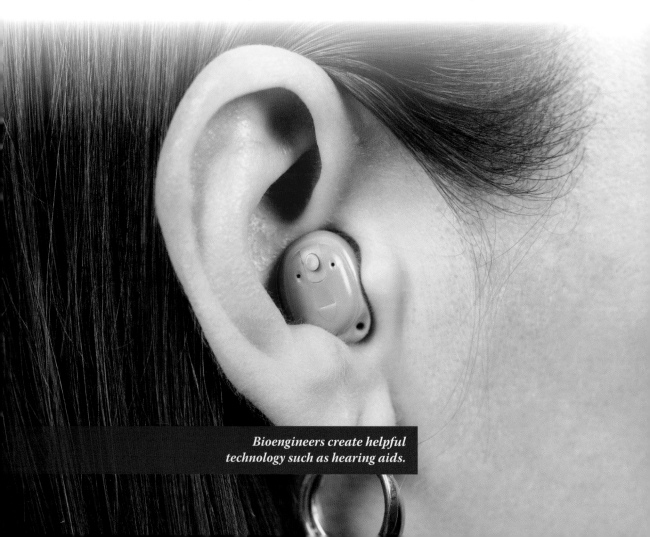

Bioengineers create helpful technology such as hearing aids.

a family member who has had a knee replaced? If so, you know someone who has benefitted from the work of bioengineers.

Bioengineers work to improve people's lives by solving many complex problems. They may work on medical, agricultural, food, energy, or environmental issues. This book focuses on the bioengineer's role in biomedicine. These scientists apply engineering **principles** to solve problems in biology and medicine. They create devices to help people with handicaps. They build new systems and instruments to **diagnose** and treat illnesses. Devices **implanted** in patients' bodies are also the work of bioengineers. Before we learn more about bioengineers, let's talk about what engineers do.

Engineers use science and mathematics to create things people need. If there is no way to travel between two islands, engineers design a bridge. If a factory needs to produce smaller cars with fewer parts, engineers will figure out the best way to do it. If the navy needs an aircraft carrier that can change direction more quickly, it's time to call in the engineers.

There are many different fields of engineering. Aerospace engineers study principles of flight, gravity, and **aerodynamics**. They use what they learn to design new airplanes and spacecraft. Petroleum engineers study rock formations and geology. They figure out the best ways to draw oil and gas from deposits deep in the earth.

Environmental engineers study the climate, wildlife, and ecology. They predict problems that might occur as cities grow larger, and they develop solutions to those problems.

Bioengineers study biology and medicine in addition to engineering. They look at how human tissue repairs itself after injury. They investigate how germs invade the body. They study human movement and measure the stress on joints during different activities.

Bioengineers use computers and other equipment to solve problems.

LEARNING & INNOVATION SKILLS

In 1816, René Laennec was a doctor with a problem. One of his patients showed signs of having a heart disease. At the time, doctors would listen to a patient's heart by pressing an ear against the patient's chest. Laennec's patient was a young woman, and he was too embarrassed to place his head against her. How could he solve this problem?

Laennec remembered something he had learned. Sound seemed to amplify as it traveled through a tube. He rolled up a sheet of paper, pressed one end against the woman's chest, and put his ear to the other end. It worked! The heart sounds came through.

This discovery led him to invent the stethoscope. This device relies on the behavior of sound waves to help medical professionals listen to heart and lung sounds. No modern-day doctor or nurse would be without one. Can you think of some other medical devices that early bioengineers might have developed?

Bioengineers also study the principles of engineering. Those with an interest in electrical engineering might study the principles of the flow of electricity through different kinds of wires. Bioengineers who are curious about civil engineering might study the principles of different building materials to see how much weight buildings can bear. Those who enjoy materials engineering might study whether metal, glass, or plastic pipes are the least likely to clog in different situations. And those who like mechanical engineering might design equipment that would be useful to other engineers.

Many medical advances have come from the work of bioengineers.

But why would bioengineers care about these things? What do electricity, building materials, clogged pipes, and equipment design have to do with biology and medicine? Plenty!

In the human body, electricity flows through nerve pathways instead of wires. Tiny electrical signals cause nerve endings to release chemicals that cause muscles to move. The skeleton is the body's support system. It bears heavy loads and suffers fractures in much the same way building materials do. Blocked blood vessels are similar to clogged plumbing. As doctors face problems that arise in our bodies' systems, they need equipment to detect and fix those problems. Doctors look to bioengineers for their help in finding solutions.

 LIFE & CAREER SKILLS

Bioengineering is serious work. But bioengineers aren't serious *all* of the time. Some bioengineers also play musical instruments or have their own bands. Others play sports in their free time. Still others like to travel to interesting places. Bioengineers know that it is important to achieve a balance between work and play.

CHAPTER TWO
ON THE JOB

Bioengineers work in all kinds of facilities. Some work in research laboratories at universities or in

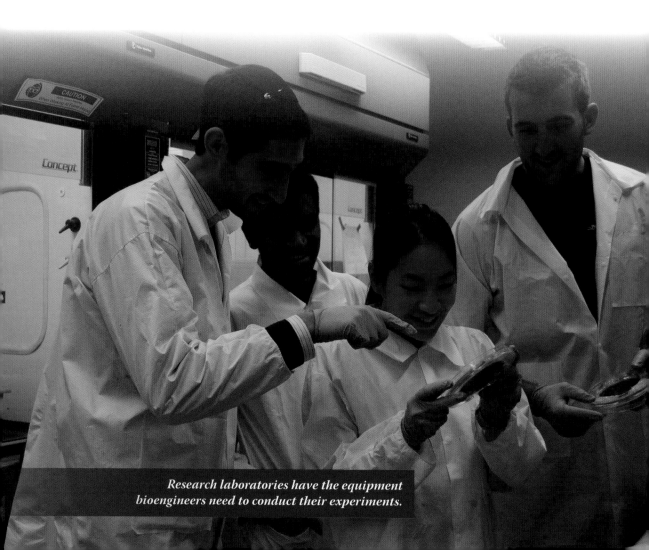

*Research laboratories have the equipment
bioengineers need to conduct their experiments.*

large companies. Others work in small companies with only two or three other engineers. Wherever they work, bioengineers use instruments such as high-powered microscopes, computers, and delicate sensing devices.

21ST CENTURY CONTENT

Most bioengineers are focused on projects related to medicine and improving human health. Some of their work, however, also benefits animals. Today, dogs receive artificial hip joints to replace bones deformed by arthritis, a painful swelling of the area where two bones are joined. Veterinarians use lasers to remove tumors from the eyes of horses. Surgeons who work with zoo animals perform operations with the help of tiny cameras.

In an indirect way, these procedures also benefit human beings. A guide dog with new, artificial hips can continue to help its blind owner. A horse with improved vision can provide many hours of exercise to its rider. In what ways would healthier animals benefit human beings?

Whether they work in a large institution or a small one, bioengineers never work alone. They always seek the advice of people who will use the devices or systems they develop. Surgeons who need tinier instruments to remove their patients' tumors will tell bioengineers the problems they have with their existing equipment. Doctors who need faster ways to run brain scans of **trauma** patients will talk to

Bioengineers need to be able to work well with other people.

Some bioengineers create tools that allow people who can't use their arms to use computers.

bioengineers about the need for speed in the emergency room. Laboratory workers who analyze blood samples might point out the steps that slow down their work.

LEARNING & INNOVATION SKILLS

People whose arms and legs are paralyzed can explain to bioengineers which everyday tasks they most need help with. Bioengineers can then design computers and pointing devices that help them to turn lights on and off, change the volume on the TV, answer the telephone, and even use e-mail. Can you think of other activities that bioengineers might be able to help these people perform? How would you design the technology to help them? How would people with paralysis operate your devices?

Much information comes from health care workers. But some bioengineers also seek the advice of patients. For instance, sports professionals can demonstrate to bioengineers the complex moves that their artificial knees or hips should be able to perform. People who have had artificial lenses implanted in their eyes can describe things that make their vision seem unnatural.

To test a new medical device, bioengineers might build it by hand. After the device is tested and improved, it can be mass-produced in a factory.

CHAPTER THREE
BECOMING
A BIOENGINEER

Bioengineers often have many interests. They are drawn to science and problem solving. They like to think

Bioengineers are usually curious about a wide variety of topics.

of better ways to do common jobs. They are interested in helping people live healthier lives. And they enjoy creating gadgets and tools that make life easier.

Bioengineers don't always plan on this career from the start. Dr. Willem Kolff, who invented the artificial kidney, or **dialysis** machine, never set out to be an inventor. As a child, he liked building things with a local carpenter. He also loved animals and wanted to be a zoo director. But Kolff's father was a doctor. Young Willem noticed how much his father worried about his patients. His dad was thrilled when they were cured, and he wept when they died. In time, Kolff knew he wanted to become a physician like his father.

Years later, Kolff treated a patient who died from kidney failure. This experience inspired Kolff to start thinking about a machine that could do the work of human kidneys. After much experimentation and many failures, he developed an artificial kidney machine that has saved many lives.

Kolff's influences were his father, his carpentry work, and his love for animals. Some bioengineers have been inspired by their early desire to help people or their concern for the safety of a relative in the military. Others have been influenced by people who have lost limbs in accidents or who have suffered with rare diseases.

A future bioengineer might be a boy who builds his own amplifier and speakers. She might be a girl who learns life-saving skills for her job as a lifeguard. Future bioengineers might also serve as volunteers in hospitals or earn Scout badges in medicine.

If you are thinking about a career in bioengineering, it is never too early to start preparing. Take classes in math and science. You might also take part in science fairs. Some schools have programs that allow students to "shadow" doctors, engineers, and other professionals. The students follow one of these professionals for a day, learning what their jobs are like.

 LIFE & CAREER SKILLS

Dr. Willem Kolff developed the artificial kidney and later worked on the artificial heart. As a young boy, he had problems in school, partly because he had dyslexia. This is a disorder that makes it difficult for people to see written words properly and to read and spell correctly. For someone in a medical or technical field, dyslexia can be a huge problem. Still, Kolff accomplished much. Could his problem with dyslexia have helped him in some way?

Science and math classes are an important part of a bioengineer's training.

In high school, you should continue your studies in math and science. You might take classes in biology, chemistry, algebra, and physics. You should also take English and writing classes, as these will help you express your ideas later on. Classes in foreign languages will help you share your ideas with other bioengineers around the world. If your school has science clubs or math competitions with other schools, these would be great activities to do.

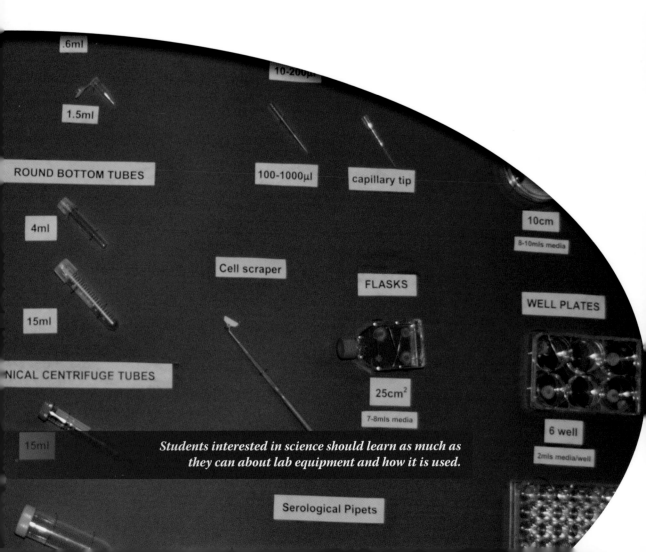

.6ml

10-200µl

1.5ml

ROUND BOTTOM TUBES

100-1000µl

capillary tip

10cm

8-10mls media

4ml

Cell scraper

FLASKS

WELL PLATES

15ml

NICAL CENTRIFUGE TUBES

25cm^2

7-8mls media

6 well

15ml

2mls media/well

Students interested in science should learn as much as they can about lab equipment and how it is used.

Serological Pipets

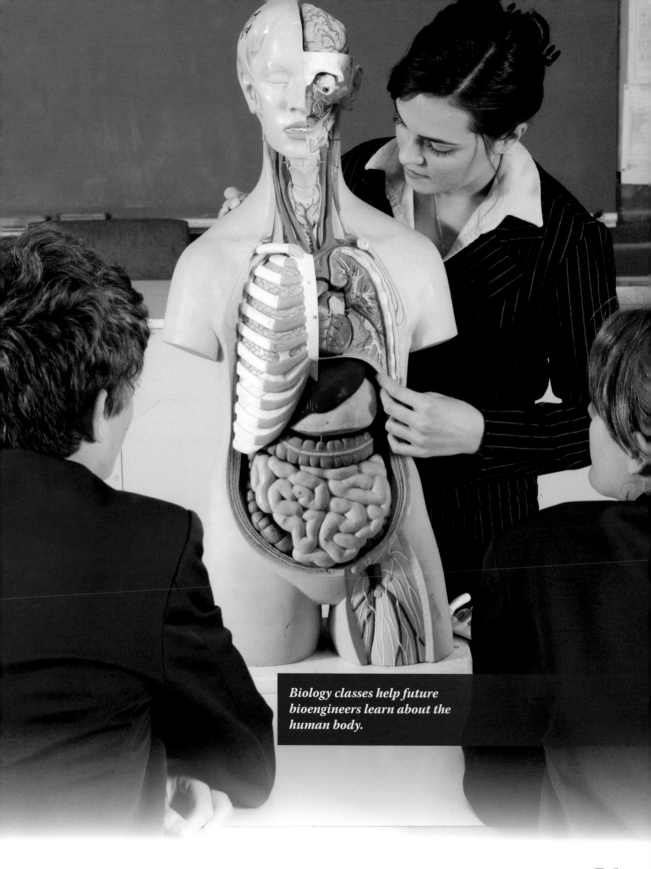

Biology classes help future bioengineers learn about the human body.

21ST CENTURY CONTENT

In 1983, about 5,000 students in the United States were working toward college degrees in bioengineering. In 2003, more than 16,000 students were working toward degrees in this field. It is likely that the demand for bioengineers will continue to increase for some time. Many people say that this is due to the aging population. How would an aging population affect the need for bioengineers?

Your college classes should also emphasize math and science. You will probably study biology, chemistry, and physics more in-depth. Your classes could include anatomy, microbiology, computer science, and calculus. You might even take engineering classes to learn about electronics, radioactive materials, or chemical production. Most careers in engineering require at least a bachelor's degree. Many fields call for a master's or doctoral degree.

You may not know your future profession when you enter college. But if you are interested in science and in helping others, you should take science courses from the very beginning. It is not unusual for future bioengineers to start out in another field entirely, only to discover their interest in bioengineering later.

College students learn the laboratory skills they will need to be skilled bioengineers.

CHAPTER FOUR
AN EXCITING FUTURE

R ight now, bioengineers are working on some amazing projects. Some are creating a "field hospital on a chip" for soldiers at war. It consists of a small sensing device that

Bioengineers will continue to make our world a better place with their work.

is worn next to the body. The device detects levels of oxygen, glucose, and other substances in the soldier's sweat. These substances can indicate whether he or she has been injured or has gone into **shock**. The information is then sent to a drug packet, also worn by the soldier. The packet releases the appropriate drugs, allowing the soldier to begin receiving treatment long before making it to a field hospital.

21ST CENTURY CONTENT

In 2000, President Bill Clinton signed a bill that created a new federal agency. It is called the National Institute of Biomedical Imaging and Bioengineering. It provides funds to help students who want to go into bioengineering. It also offers a newsletter that keeps bioengineers up-to-date on the latest advances in the field.

A number of bioengineers are working to help people avoid hip and spine fractures in old age. They are studying bone tissues to see why they lose their strength. They want to figure out whether the tissues can be prompted to form strong, new cells instead.

Some bioengineers are working to create artificial organs. Real organs are formed by different structures and tissue layers. Scientists take human cells and attempt to guide their growth to match these structures and tissue layers. In the future, new drugs might be tested on these artificial organs.

LIFE & CAREER SKILLS

Professor Heinz Wolff of the United Kingdom has spent all of his adult life in scientific pursuits. He has worked in medical research, studied problems with weightlessness in space, and developed technology to help the disabled and elderly. He even invented the term *bioengineering*.

Wolff strives to show young people how exciting and fun science can be. He often appears on British radio and television shows with amazing stories of scientific problems and bioengineered solutions. Professor Wolff feels strongly that people should think about the social and moral **consequences** of advances in science. What might some of those consequences be?

Bioengineers use microfabrication and nanofabrication methods to mimic the function of human organs on a chip.

Bioengineers are also developing ever more delicate surgical tools. They are designing lasers, tiny cameras, and other instruments. These help surgeons to operate inside the eyeball, deep in the ear canal, and even inside microscopic blood vessels.

Bioengineering is an exciting field. Bioengineers are creative, clever people who are fascinated with science and who love to solve problems. They are remarkable men and women who use their skills and talents to improve people's lives.

What exciting discoveries will bioengineers make next?

SOME WELL-KNOWN BIOENGINEERS

Takuo Aoyagi (1936–) is a Japanese engineer who discovered how to measure the level of oxygen in a patient's blood. His development of pulse **oximetry** allows doctors to notice when patients are low on oxygen. It has led to a significant drop in deaths during surgery.

Y. C. "Bert" Fung (1919–) is known as the Father of Modern **Biomechanics**. His work has led to improvements in the understanding of diabetes, high blood pressure, the formation of blood clots, and the characteristics of cancer cells.

Robert Langer (1948–) developed polymeric drug delivery materials and devices to control the amount of medicine present in a patient's system.

Robert W. Mann (1924–2006) worked to help people with disabilities. Perhaps his best-known invention was the Boston Arm for amputees. This **electromechanical** arm is powered by signals from the remaining muscles.

Gail K. Naughton (1955–) helped develop new ways to grow human tissues outside of the body. This technology helps patients with heart disease, cancer, and many other illnesses heal in more effective, less painful ways.

Frank Pantridge (1916–2004) was an Irish-born **cardiologist** who developed the portable defibrillator. This device delivers a shock to restore a normal rhythm to a heart that is not functioning properly.

Ioannis Yannas (1935–) is the co-inventor and developer of human "artificial skin," which is used to treat burn patients. The new skin is grown on a small **scaffold** with starter cells from the patients themselves.

GLOSSARY

aerodynamics (air-oh-dy-NAM-iks) the branch of science that deals with the movement of objects through air and other gases

biomechanics (by-oh-muh-KAN-iks) the study of the mechanical nature of biological activities such as the beating of the heart and movement of fluids

cardiologist (kar-dee-AH-luh-jist) a doctor who specializes in treating patients with heart disease

consequences (KON-suh-kwen-sez) outcomes or results

diagnose (DY-uhg-nohss) to decide what disease is present based on the symptoms experienced

dialysis (dy-AL-uh-sis) the process by which impurities in the blood are removed

electromechanical (ih-LEK-tro-muh-KAN-ih-kuhl) having mechanical, or moving, parts that are run by electricity

implanted (im-PLAN-ted) inserted inside the human body

oximetry (ahk-SIM-ih-tree) the measurement of how much oxygen is in the blood

principles (PRIN-suh-puhlz) basic, general laws or truths

scaffold (SKAF-uhld) a framework upon which biological tissues can grow

shock (SHAHK) a medical emergency that is common after a severe injury in which there is a sudden decrease in blood flow through the body

trauma (TRAW-muh) a severe injury

FOR MORE INFORMATION

BOOKS

Gray, Susan H. *Artificial Limbs*. Ann Arbor, MI: Cherry Lake Publishing, 2009.

Jeffrey, Gary. *Medical Breakthroughs*. New York: Rosen Central, 2008.

Snedden, Robert. *Medical Technology*. Mankato, MN: Smart Apple Media, 2009.

WEB SITES

Engineer Your Life
www.engineeryourlife.org/
Read about women engineers and learn more about engineering careers.

Engineering in Medicine and Biology—Designing a Career in Biomedical Engineering
www.embs.org/docs/careerguide.pdf
Read an excellent introduction to the work of bioengineers and how to prepare for the profession.

NIBIB—Science Education
www.nibib.nih.gov/HealthEdu/ScienceEdu
Discover news and information for students from the National Institute of Biomedical Imaging and Bioengineering.

Sloan Career Cornerstone Center—Bioengineering Overview
www.careercornerstone.org/pdf/bioeng/bioeng.pdf
Learn about the field of bioengineering and ways to plan for entering the profession.

INDEX

ABOUT THE AUTHOR

Susan H. Gray has a master's degree in zoology. She has taught college-level courses in biology, anatomy, and physiology. She has also written more than 120 science and reference books for children. In her free time, she likes to garden and play the piano. Susan lives in Cabot, Arkansas, with her husband, Michael, and many pets.